12/16/09

Sugar Grove Library
Sugar Grove, Il 60554
www.sugargrove.lib.il.us
1-630-466-4686

DISCARDED

kid STARS!

Abigail Breslin

Katherine Rawson

Sugar Grove Library
Sugar Grove, Il 60554
www.sugargrove.lib.il.us
1-630-466-4686

PowerKiDS press
New York

Published in 2010 by The Rosen Publishing Group, Inc.
29 East 21st Street, New York, NY 10010

Copyright © 2010 by The Rosen Publishing Group, Inc.

All rights reserved. No part of this book may be reproduced in any form without permission in writing from the publisher, except by a reviewer.

First Edition

Editor: Nicole Pristash
Book Design: Kate Laczynski
Book Layout: Julio Gil
Photo Researcher: Jessica Gerweck

Photo Credits: Cover Frank Micelotta/Getty Images for Nickelodeon; p. 4 © Andrew Marks/Corbis; p. 7 Stephen Lovekin/Getty Images; p. 8 © Touchstone Pictures/Zuma Press, Inc.; p. 11 Lee Celano/WireImage/Getty Images; p. 12 © Fox Searchlight Pictures/Zuma Press, Inc.; p. 15 © Mario Anzuoni/Reuters/Corbis; p. 16 © Universal Pictures/Zuma Press, Inc.; p. 12 Michael Caulfield/Stand Up To Cancer via Getty Images; p. 20 © Katy Winn/Corbis.

Library of Congress Cataloging-in-Publication Data

Rawson, Katherine.
  Abigail Breslin / Katherine Rawson. — 1st ed.
    p. cm. — (Kid stars!)
  Includes index.
  ISBN 978-1-4042-8146-2 (library binding) — ISBN 978-1-4358-3412-5 (pbk.) — ISBN 978-1-4358-3413-2 (6-pack)
  1. Breslin, Abigail, 1996– —Juvenile literature. 2. Actors—United States—Biography—Juvenile literature. I. Title.
  PN2287.B6855R39 2010
  791.4302'8092—dc22
  [B]

2009011664

Manufactured in the United States of America

Contents

Meet Abigail Breslin 5
An Early Start 6
Her First Movie 9
Bigger Roles 10
Little Miss Sunshine 13
Award Winner 14
Nim and Kit 17
Abigail's Life 18
What's Next? 21
Fun Facts 22
Glossary 23
Index 24
Web Sites 24

Many of the actors Abigail has worked with have said that she is one of the best young actresses around.

Meet Abigail Breslin

Abigail Breslin is probably best known for the part she played in *Little Miss Sunshine*. However, Abigail has been in a lot of other movies. You may also know her from the movies *Nim's Island* and *Kit Kittredge: An American Girl*. She has appeared on TV, too!

Abigail began acting when she was just three years old. She starred in her first movie when she was only five. Abigail is young, but she is very talented. She is going to go far in Hollywood. Let's take a look at how Abigail got her start and find out what makes her such a great star.

An Early Start

Abigail Kathleen Breslin was born in New York City on April 14, 1996. She is named after Abigail Adams. Abigail Adams was the wife of John Adams, the second president of the United States. Abigail's mother and father are Kim and Mike Breslin. She has two older brothers, Ryan and Spencer. Spencer is also an actor.

Abigail got her first acting job when she was three years old. She was in a **commercial** for Toys "R" Us, a toy store. Even though she was so young, Abigail liked acting. She knew that she wanted to continue doing it.

Abigail (left) and her brother Spencer (right) are like most brothers and sisters. They generally get along, but Abigail says that they have moments when they do not.

In *Signs*, Abigail (right) got to work with big stars, such as Mel Gibson (left), Joaquin Phoenix (center left), and Rory Culkin (seated).

Her First Movie

When Abigail was five years old, she starred in the movie *Signs*. *Signs* is about a family who faces visitors from another **planet**. Abigail plays the daughter, Bo. *Signs* is a scary movie, but Abigail had a good time working on it. "Everyone was just so nice," she said.

Many people who watched *Signs* saw how talented Abigail was. Soon, she was given roles, or parts, as a guest star on some TV shows. A guest star is someone who appears on a show but does not become part of the cast. In 2002, Abigail guest starred on *Hack* and *What I Like About You*.

Bigger Roles

Abigail soon got bigger parts in movies. In 2004, she starred in *Raising Helen*. Abigail's brother Spencer starred in this movie, too. They played a brother and sister. In the movie, Abigail's and Spencer's characters have to go live with their aunt Helen because their mother and father have died. Helen has trouble at first, but she learns how to take care of the kids.

One of Abigail's next movies was *Chestnut: Hero of Central Park*, in which she plays an **orphan** again. In the movie, Abigail's character and another orphan must hide their dog Chestnut from their new family in New York City.

This picture shows Spencer (bottom left) and Abigail (bottom right) with their cast mates at *Raising Helen*'s first showing in Los Angeles in May 2004.

This is a scene from *Little Miss Sunshine* in which Abigail's character, Olive, comforts her brother Dwayne (right). Dwayne was played by actor Paul Dano.

Little Miss Sunshine

In 2005, when she was nine years old, Abigail played a part in a movie that would make her a big star. That movie was *Little Miss Sunshine*. Abigail plays Olive, a girl who is picked to be in a **beauty pageant**. The movie is about the road trip that Olive and her strange family take to get to the pageant and what happens once they get there.

When the cast was making the film, Abigail's co-stars were surprised at how good at acting she was despite her age. Abigail's hard work in the movie paid off. The movie became a big hit.

Award Winner

Little Miss Sunshine was one of the most popular movies of 2006. The movie got very good **reviews**, and Abigail got a lot of attention for her acting in it. She was even **nominated** for an Academy **Award**! An Academy Award is one of the biggest awards an actor can get. She did not win it, but she did win a Young Artist Award in 2007.

Little Miss Sunshine made Abigail very famous, but she still tries to live a **normal** life. "My friends do not treat me any differently because I am famous," she has said.

On January 12, 2007, Abigail won the Critics' Choice Award for best young actress. Here she is shown getting the award in Santa Monica, California.

In this scene from *Nim's Island*, Abigail's character, Nim, is dancing with a sea lion named Selkie. Abigail liked working with the sea lions because they gave her kisses!

Nim and Kit

Abigail's success led to parts in some fun movies. In 2008, she starred in *Nim's Island*. In this movie, she plays Nim, a girl who lives on a magical island. While making the movie, Abigail got to work with animals, such as a sea lion and a lizard. She said she loved working with all the animals except the bugs!

Abigail then starred in *Kit Kittredge: An American Girl*. This movie takes place in the 1930s. "I got to learn so much about history in a very real way," Abigail said. To play Kit, Abigail had to wear a wig and have freckles painted on her!

Abigail's Life

Acting is hard work, and it takes up a lot of time. Abigail does not go to school because of her busy acting **schedule**. Instead, Abigail is homeschooled. She also studies for 3 hours every day.

In her free time, Abigail likes to do different things. She enjoys swimming and reading. She also likes to talk on the phone and make art. Like most young girls, Abigail likes to spend time with her friends, too. She enjoys doing the same things that most girls enjoy. Abigail is a famous actress, but acting is only one part of her life.

Abigail (left) enjoys raising money for those in need. Here she is seen at Stand Up To Cancer, a charity event held in Los Angeles, in 2008.

Abigail (center) has said that when she is recognized, her fans are really nice. Here she is shown spending time with some fans in Los Angeles.

What's Next?

In 2009, Abigail starred in *My Sister's Keeper*. In the movie, she plays Anna, a girl who has the power to save her dying sister.

Even though Abigail is so young, she is one of the most talented actresses around. She enjoys playing different parts. "What I like about it is being a different person," she has said. Abigail wants to continue acting, but she also hopes to go to **college** some day. Her fans, though, hope she will not stop acting anytime soon. Abigail has proven that she can play many types of characters. We hope to see her play even more!

ABIGAIL BRESLIN

 Abigail's friends and family call her Abbie.

 Pizza and cupcakes are two of her **favorite** foods.

 Abigail likes American Girl dolls, and she owns several.

 She loves to read.

 When Abigail picks parts to play, she thinks about whether they are characters that she would like to know in real life.

 She has two dogs, a cat, and a turtle.

 Abigail is a member of the Girl Scouts of the USA, a youth group for girls.

 *Finding Nemo* is one of her favorite movies.

 Abigail said that if she were a superhero, she would want the power to fly and to be able to speak every language.

 She is friends with Dakota Fanning, another famous young actress.

Glossary

award (uh-WAWRD) A special honor given to someone.

beauty pageant (BYOO-tee PA-jent) A show in which judges pick the most beautiful women or girls.

college (KO-lij) A place where people can continue to study after high school.

commercial (kuh-MER-shul) A TV message that tries to sell something.

favorite (FAY-vuh-rut) Most liked.

nominated (NAH-muh-nayt-ed) Suggested that you be given an award.

normal (NOR-mul) Regular.

orphan (OR-fun) A child who no longer has a mother or a father.

planet (PLA-net) A large object, such as Earth, that moves around the Sun or another star.

popular (PAH-pyuh-lur) Liked by lots of people.

reviews (rih-VYOOZ) Written opinions that list something's good and bad points.

schedule (SKEH-jool) A plan of what one has to do at certain times.

Index

A
Academy Award, 14
actress(es), 5, 18, 21–22

B
beauty pageant, 13

C
college, 21
commercial, 6

H
Hollywood, 5

K
Kit Kittredge: An American Girl, 5, 17

L
Little Miss Sunshine, 5, 13–14

M
movie(s), 5, 9–10, 13–14, 17, 21–22

N
New York City, 6, 10
Nim's Island, 5, 17

T
TV, 5

Web Sites

Due to the changing nature of Internet links, PowerKids Press has developed an online list of Web sites related to the subject of this book. This site is updated regularly. Please use this link to access the list:
www.powerkidslinks.com/kids/breslin/

Sugar Grove Library
Sugar Grove, Il 60554
www.sugargrove.lib.il.us
1-630-466-4686